God Made Me Special
Children's Devotional

Written by
Adassa Wright

Adassa's Outlet

https://adassasoutlet.com

God Made Me Special (Children's Devotional)

© 2023 Adassa Wright

Your voice is extremely valuable to me. If your child enjoyed this book, and you would like to let others know about it, please take a moment to leave a heartfelt review at the store you made your purchase. Thank you so much in advance for your time.

Written by Adassa Wright

ISBN: 979-8-9874534-2-1

Library of Congress Control Number: 2023900070

Printed in the United States of America

This Book Belongs

To:

_____

_____

From:

_____

_____

_____

The earth was without form and void; darkness was upon the face of the deep.

And the Spirit of God moved upon the face of the water.

And God said, "Let there be light," and there was light. God saw that the light was good. The evening and the morning were the first day. Genesis 1:1-4 (KJV)

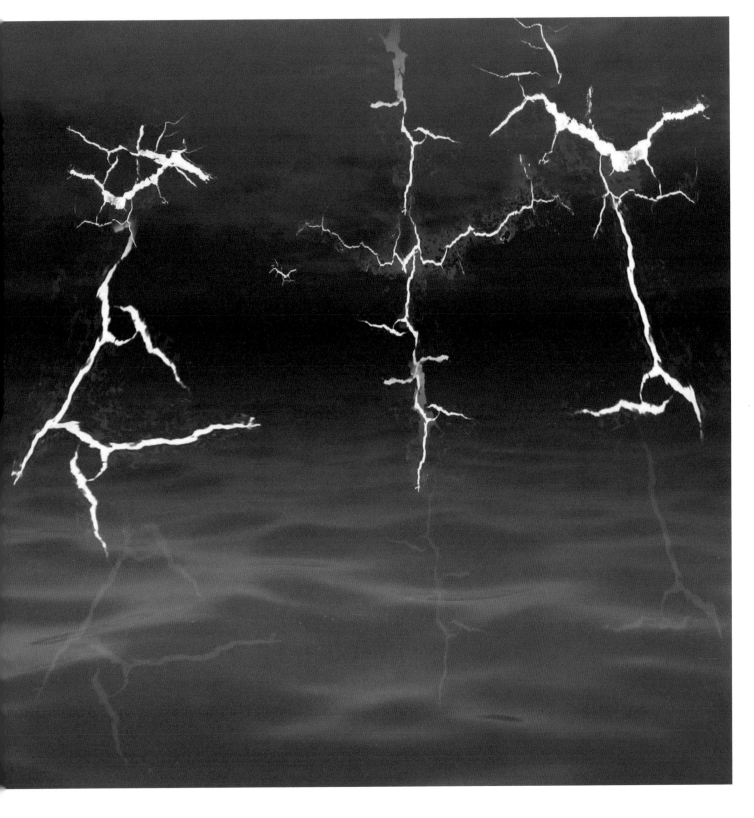

Jesus said, "I am the light of the world."
John 8:12 (KJV) Let your light shine before men that they may see your good works and glorify your father, which is in heaven. Matthew 5:16 (KJV)

Glorify God in all that you do: share a toy, a book, or your lunch with someone. A friendly smile could bring joy to someone's heart. Kind words are uplifting, you're special, Jesus loves you, good morning, thank you, please...
Give a helping hand to your mother, teacher, or friends. Be a reflection of Jesus! Shine!

And God said, let there be a firmament, and he called the firmament heaven. And the evening and the morning were the second day.

God said, "let the waters under the heaven gathered together in one place and let dryland appear," and it was so. Genesis 1:7-9 (KJV)
God called the dry land earth. He called the waters seas. And God saw that it was good. Wow! Miraculous God, Amen!

And God said, "Let the earth bring forth grass, the herb yielding seed, and the fruit tree yielding fruits after his kind," and it was so. God saw that it was good. "And the evening and the morning were the third day." Genesis 1: 11 &13.

Praise the Lord for providing plants and all the delicious fruits, Amen!

God made two brilliant lights, the sun and the moon. He said, "let them be for signs and for seasons, and for days and years." Genesis 1:14-18 (KJV)

God made the greater light to rule the day.
I have fun during the day when I learn and play.
He made the lesser light to rule the night, and he made the stars as well. He called the darkness night. The evening and the morning were the fourth day.

I love you, Lord, for making light. I sleep
and grow at night.
Good night God, I am going to bed. Amen!

God said, "let the water bring forth living creatures," the great whales, octopus, sharks, and all the fishes in the sea. Genesis 1:20-22.

And Jesus said, "Follow me, and I will make you fishers of men." Jesus invited Simon Peter and his brother Andrew, fishers and made them into fishers of men. He made them into disciples so they would make disciples of others. They left their nets and followed Jesus. I am ready to follow Jesus! Are you? Matthew 4:18-20 (KJV)

God made the land produce living creatures according to their kind: the cattle, gorillas, lions, elephants, alligators, lizards and all the other animals. And God saw that it was good. Mighty is our God! Hallelujah!

"Every kind of beasts, and birds, and of serpents, and of things in the sea is tamed of mankind: But the tongue can no man tame." James 3:7-8 Be truthful and kind with your words. Proverbs18:21 (KJV) says, "Life and death are in the power of the tongue." Speak life!

The Lord God made the fowls that fly above the earth: the eagles, the parrots, the doves, the hummingbirds, and every feathered and winged birds: ostriches, flamingos, peacocks, you name them, God made them. You're an amazing God! Amen!

The evening and the morning were the fifth day. Isaiah 40:31 says, "But they that wait upon the Lord shall renew their strength; they shall mount up with wings as eagles; they shall run and not be weary; and they shall walk, and not faint." I'm going to wait on you Lord and increase in strength. I'll soar like an eagle!

And God said, "let us make man in our image, after our likeness." Let them have dominion over all that I have created.
The Lord God formed man out of the dust of the ground and breathed into his nostrils and man became a living soul." Genesis 1:26-28 (KJV)

You and I are God's masterpiece! We are made in the image of God.
Read the following aloud: I am fearfully and wonderfully made.
God made mommy and daddy and me. Thank you, Lord for the breath of life! How excellent is thy name Lord God! Amen!

The heaven and the earth were finished and all that was in it. God made the fruits, seeds and vegetables for our food. God made food for man and beast. Yes, the elephant, giraffe, and goats are herbivores. They eat plants, fruits, seeds and vegetables and they are big and strong.

Let us eat so we can be healthy, strong and beautiful.

Thank you, Lord, for the food we eat, amen!

God gave man dominion to rule over the fish of the sea, and over the fowl of the air, and over the cattle, and over all the earth, and over every creeping thing that creeps upon the earth.

God created male and female, and he blessed them and said unto them be fruitful, and multiply, and replenish the earth. Genesis 1:28 (KJV)

God has given us every herb bearing plant and every tree that has fruit with seed in it for our food and for the beasts, the birds in the sky and the creatures that move along the ground, everything that has breath of life God, has given the green plant for food. Genesis 1:29-30 (KJV)

The evening and the morning were the sixth day. Trust God, he created us and provided an abundance of all that we need; he knows what is best for us. Eat and enjoy moderate servings of the goodness God has provided. Thank you, Lord for providing! Amen!

God saw all that he had made, and it was very good. Amazing God!
He separated the waters, sea, rivers, and land. Amazing King!
He made the sun and the moon for signs and for seasons, and for days and years. Creator of everything, man and beast.

Let's follow the master's plan, he made provision and a system to sustain life before he created man and beast. Praise the all-wise God, Hallelujah!

"On the seventh day God ended his work which he had made, and he rested on the seventh day from all his work." "God blessed the seventh day and sanctified it."
Genesis 2:2(KJV)

Thank you, Lord, for a day of rest. Let us worship our creator and our King. Mighty is our God! Hallelujah!

God prepared a beautiful home for Adam called the Garden of Eden.

God put the man in the garden to care for it and he also presented all the animals to him, and he named them. Genesis 2:19 20 (KJV)

God gave man chores and assignments. Whatever your hand finds to do, do it with all your might... Ecclesiastes 9:10 (KJV)

The Lord God said, "it is not good that the man should be alone," so he caused the man to fall in a deep sleep and took one of his ribs and closed-up the flesh.
The Lord God used the rib to make a woman and brought her unto Adam to be his wife.
Genesis 2:21-22 (KJV)

God placed Adam and his wife, Eve, in a beautiful garden called Eden to dress it and to keep it.
Here we have the first marriage, the first family, and the first home. Created and blessed by God.

When I consider thy heavens, the work of thy fingers, the moon, and the stars, which thou have ordained; what is man? Thou made him to have dominion over the works of thy hands. O Lord our Lord, how excellent is thy name in all the earth. Psalm 8:3, 4 & 9 (KJV)

Holy! holy! holy! Lord God Almighty...
Thou art worthy, O Lord, to receive glory and honor and power: for thou have created all things, and for thy pleasure they are and were created. Amen!
Revelation 4:11 (KJV)

ABOUT THE AUTHOR

Adassa Wright is passionate about children's education. She loves her family, animals and nature but above all, she loves the Lord. She taught children in her household and community, which inspired her to earn a bachelor's degree in Education from Northern Caribbean University, Manchester, Jamaica.

After spending over twenty years teaching young children, she understands the importance of the formative years. These are the years that define who a child is and who they will become in the future. She became inspired to write books for children that inspire confidence and give them the assurance that we love them. They are valuable, beautiful, strong, and that Jesus loves them unconditionally. The primary aim of this book is to change the world one child at a time. She also hopes that this book encourages parents to be intentional and consistent as they reinforce the love and appreciation for God, love for others and love for oneself, giving their children the greatest gift of all, love.

She can be contacted at info@adassasoutlet.com

Printed in Great Britain
by Amazon

37272658R00021